....und er ist doch ein Monster!

Textsammlung

Autoren: Dirk L. und Tanja M. Feiler

Bilder: Dirk L. und Tanja M. Feiler

Cover: Tanja M. Feiler

Vorwort

Im Juni 2013 hat mein Mann, Dirk L. Feiler, Buchautor, Publisher zum ersten Mal Post vom Presidenten der USA erhalten, kurz später von seiner Frau, White House, ehem. Presidenten und vielen mehr. Barack Obama hat um Hilfe gebeten und mein Mann und ich haben natürlich geholfen. Doch jetzt hat sich herauskristallisiert, zu welchen Handlungen dieser Mann fähig ist und wie er die Menschen abzockt.

Von Tanja M. Feiler

Kapitel I Die eine Seite – Die Wut

Guten Abend, ich lebe - jetzt helfen Sie mir bitte auch einmal - Halten Sie mir diesen Barack Obama Mittelname: Husein vom Leib, dieser Mensch terrorisiert und macht mich - Er ist Krank - veranlassen Sie eine Untersuchung - Der Mann hat mich «Zwangsterilissiren» lassen. Er schreibt mir Emails - "Ich weis wer dich Gebaut hat" dass ist ja wohl nur krank - Er hat mich 80 mal angeschrieben und dann eine Warnung wenn ich nicht zahle, von meiner Grundsicherung - dann kann es Passieren das Menschen unter einer

Eisfläche verschwinden. Er hat mir seit 2009 mehrere Billionen gestohlen.

Leiten Sie eine Untersuchung ein. Dieser Mann ist sehr krank!

Klären Sie diesen Fall auf. Ansonsten wende ich mich an die Menschenrechte - Organisationen.

Ich werde in allem weiterhin helfen. Sie wissen, Sie haben kein Anrecht auf mein Geld - Guten haben Frau Angela Merkel

Schreiben Sie mich an wenn Sie von mir Informationen brauchen oder meiner Frau.

Nehmen dieses Ernst.

Dirk Leopold Feiler

Der Account bleibt geöffnet.

Danke

Obama - beende diesen Scheiß - Du bist ein Schwein mehr nicht. Komm selbst Du kleiner Wixer - diese Sprache ist die einzige die Du verstehst.

Lerne Deutsch und stottre am Telefon nicht herum. Dummheit macht mir Angst und Du bist mehr als Dumm- Du brauchst ärztliche Hilfe.

Ich wollte eine Familie gründen! Soll ich Dir das lesen beibringen. Massenmörder.

Hop´ Freund - auf geht´s ich werde keine Geduld aufbringen ("Seniorpartner B. H. Obama")

Freund - Ich werde Deine Schuld beweisen - weil ich vergeben kann. .

Und meine Aktie hast Du auch gestohlen. Freundchen - Du bist nicht inteligent! (Wenn ich nur schon von Dir höre niemals vergeben) Im Jahre 2009.

Ich warte 10 Minuten - dann will Geld auf meinem Konto sehen - sollte dass nicht passieren schmeiss ich Dich bei DLFV raus. Ab Jetzt: + - 10 Minuten höchstens + 5 Minuten! dirk.feiler@yahoo.de - Pay Pal.

Wenn Du leben willst mein Freund dann schaff die Todesstrafe ab. Du tust es für Dich!

Wir verstehen uns wenn ich das will - lerne das WORT WILL - eigener WILLE. Oder ich werde es tun !!! Kapiert. Du darfst das weise Hause behalten Sohn - wenn Du Deine Arbeit erledigst. Wer dagegen ist kann ja drüber plauderen. Kev - den Hosenscheisser musste ich mal ins kalte Wasser werfen.

Barack - ich werde gleich schauen und dann werde ich Dich erst einmal aus meinem Verlag hinausbefördern.

Kapitel 2. Die andere Seite

Wir Kinder Dieser Erde BY Dirk L. Feiler ...

hat mir eine sehr interessante Freundschaft beschert - die des US Presidenten President Barack Obama.

Michelle Obama nannte mich das Herz und Seele Amerikas. Michelle Obama nannte mich das Herz und Seele Amerikas. Ich fühlte mich als! DEUTSCHER mehr als geehrt und ich werde den Präsidenten den „Rest" seiner Amtszeit begleiten. Nie im Leben hätte ich gedacht das mich einmal ein US President um Hilfe bittet.

Danke - ich werde das Globalsozial
RICHTIGE tun.

Best in Teen; Fiction; Nonfiction; BAM!
Praesident Pick.

Ich hoffe wir werden noch viel Gutes
erreichen

Von Dirk L. Feiler

Kapitell 3. Post an Tanja M. Feiler vom Presidenten der vereinigten Staaten

Barack Obama

Do this for me, Tanja

An ich Jan 31 um 6:00 PM

Tanja, right now we're seeing how everything we've fought for together is making the State of our Union stronger.

Our economy is creating jobs at a faster pace than any other year since the '90s. Unemployment is currently lower than it was before the financial crisis began. More of our children are graduating than ever before, more people are getting affordable health care than ever before, and we're relying on less foreign oil than we have in almost three decades.

These policies continue to work because they are based on the same commonsense principles that we've always held deep in our hearts, Tanja -- values that consider the needs of every American, and every community. Ideas that are at the core of who we are as Democrats.

So I hope that you're as proud as I am to be a member of our party. If so, then I need you to represent

Democrats everywhere you go, Tanja, because our unity is how we carry our success through 2015 and beyond. That's why I want to make sure you pitch in $10 or more before midnight -- to support the work that we're doing, and to get your official Democratic Party membership card in the mail as well.

If you've saved your payment information, your donation will go through immediately.

QUICK DONATE: $10

QUICK DONATE: $25

QUICK DONATE: $50

QUICK DONATE: $100

QUICK DONATE: $200

Or donate another amount.

After six years you're still standing with me, and I'll always appreciate you. I may not have any more elections to win, but there's still plenty more work for you and me to get done.

So Tanja, let's finish this together. Chip in $10 or more before midnight tonight, so you can get your membership card:

https://my.democrats.org/Become-a-2015-Member

Thanks for everything,

Barack Obama

Kapitel 4: Post an Tanja M. Feiler von der First Lady, Michelle Obama

You've earned your membership card

Michelle Obama

An ich Jan 30 um 3:19 PM

Friend --

At the end of the day there are so many ways you show your commitment as a Democrat.

You've supported my husband through the past six years -- when we've celebrated, and when we've had to regroup. You've helped your fellow Democrats stay inspired, and you've remembered our principles when we've been confronted with adversity.

Thank you.

That's why I want to make sure you have the chance to get your 2015 DNC membership card.

It's so easy. Just donate $10 or more to the party via the links below, and the DNC will send you your new membership card in the mail. (It has a picture of Barack on it -- so I'm a fan.)

Take advantage of this right now!

If you've saved your payment information, your donation will go through immediately.

QUICK DONATE: $10

QUICK DONATE: $25

QUICK DONATE: $50

QUICK DONATE: $100

QUICK DONATE: $200

Or donate another amount:

https://my.democrats.org/Become-a-2015-Member

What happens this year is entirely in your hands. That's why I'm so optimistic.

Sincerely,

Michelle

This email was sent to melfuller20@yahoo.com. If this isn't the best email address at which to reach you, update your contact information. Our email list is the best way we have of staying in regular contact with supporters like you across the country and letting you know about the work President

Obama and other Democrats are doing. If you like staying in touch, but want to receive only the most important messages, click here. Click here to unsubscribe from our supporter list, but if you leave, it will be harder for you to stay involved in the organization that you've been such a critical part of. This organization is powered by you, and we'd love to hear your ideas. Send us any comments, criticisms, or feedback here, or just reply to this email! Thanks for supporting President Obama and other Democrats.

Post der First Lady an Tanja M. Feiler

The most important story:

First Lady Michelle Obama

An   ich 19. Jan

WhiteHouse.gov/SOTU

Tomorrow night, Barack will deliver his sixth State of the Union address.

That means tonight, he'll be sitting down at his desk, reviewing each and every word to make sure his speech tells the most important story: yours.

For Barack, that is what this address is about. Not politics or partisanship, but the lives you lead, the challenges you face, and the future you hope to build for yourself and for your children. Every day, he reads those stories in the letters folks send to him from across the country.

Barack sat down to talk about what makes the address so personal for him, and what will make 2015 special.

Make sure you watch the video -- then join me and millions of other Americans on Tuesday in watching the State of the Union.

I have the honor of watching Tuesday's speech with a few of the inspiring Americans who shared their story with Barack this year.

Anthony Mendez overcame every obstacle put in his way to become the first member of his family to graduate high school. Carolyn Reed opened her third sub shop in Colorado with help from a federal small business loan -- she and her husband now own seven. Victor Fugate worked hard to bounce back from unemployment, earn his degree, and find a job. Jason Gibson returned from Afghanistan without either of his legs. Today, he is recovering and his wife just gave birth to a baby girl.

Their grit and dedication represent what's best about this country, and while we have made so much progress, we have so much left to do to make sure all Americans have the opportunities they deserve to get ahead. That's what my husband will be talking about tomorrow.

So go to WhiteHouse.gov/SOTU, watch the President reflect on this year's address, then tune in tomorrow at 9 p.m ET.

Thanks,

First Lady Michelle Obama

Kapitel 5: Friend Merk Dir das!

Mein Mann und ich haben zusammen inzwischen über 40 Bücher veröffentlicht, in denen natürlich ein Großteil der Post, die wir von OFA, White House, dem Presidenten und seiner Frau sowie anderen erhalten haben veröffentlicht ist.

Besonders Danke ich meinem Ehemann